Fathers

Collected Poems 1973-2015

KEN KOPROWSKI

Fathers: Collected Poems 1973 - 2015

by Ken Koprowski

Published by White Stag
(An Imprint of Ravenswood Publishing)

December 2015

Grateful acknowledgement is made to the following periodicals in which some of these poems first appeared: *Lamp in the Spine, Lorax, Stash, Syracuse Poems, Wetlands, The Carlton Miscellaney.*

Ravenswood Publishing
Autryville, NC 28318
http://www.ravenswoodpublishing.com

Printed in the U.S.A.

ISBN-13: 978-0692734827
ISBN-10: 0692734821

Credits

Cover photo: (From rear) Grandsons Ken, Tony and Steve Koprowski on the back porch of the Krysiak homestead -- St. Augustine Street, Pulaski, WI, 1954.
Photo Credit: Eugene Krysiak

My thanks photo credit: Ken Koprowski

War Department letter page 10: Anne Krysiak Anderson

Photo page 14: French Fourragere (green and red)
Credit: "Fourragère CG" by davric - collection personnelle. Licensed under Public Domain via Wikimedia Commons

Photo page 39: Steve Koprowski and Jacob Koprowski, 1974
Credit: Ken Koprowski

Photo page 54: Steve, Ken and Tony peeking from the mulberry tree beside the Krysiak family homestead, circa 1957.
Credit: Eugene Krysiak

About the Author photo credit: Pamela A. Koprowski

Dedication

Think for a minute how you came to be who you are.

Why do you twiddle your thumbs when you're bored?
Why do you love the deep woods no matter the season?
Why are your children the most important people, especially when they irritate you?
Why do you miss your grandfather so much that his memory brings tears 40 years after his passing?

Fathers.

Good and bad, they make sons and grandsons, students and acolytes the fathers we become.
Thank God for the ones who inspire with unqualified love and praise.
The ones who teach with honesty and integrity.
The ones who break Grandma's rules to have fun and a beer.
They are saving the world with our Mothers, who knew how to do this all along.

Thank you, Stanley Krysiak for your enduring, unqualified love. And thank you Victoria Krysiak for understanding and letting us play.

Thank you Mom and Dad for sending me north so often with my "Polish American twin." This book is dedicated to all of you with my love.

Contents

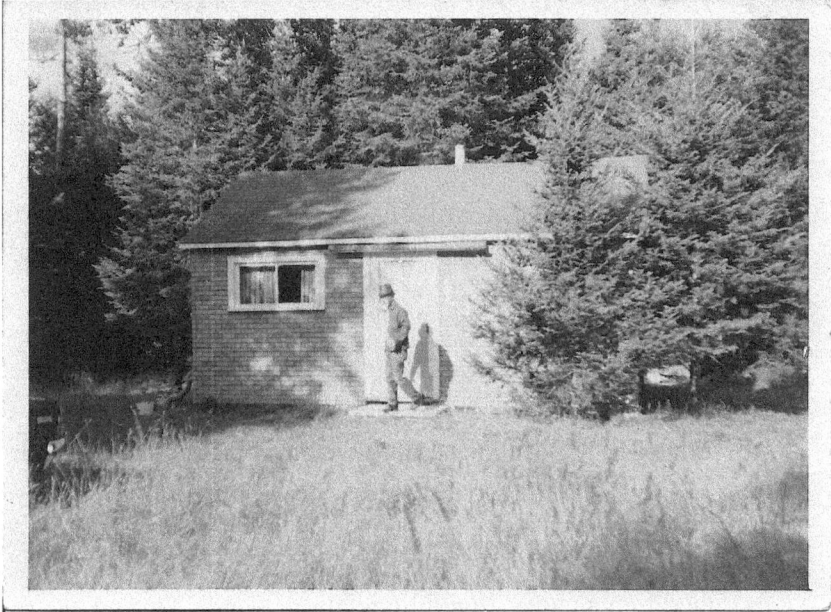

Stanley Krysiak, 76, at his hunting cabin in Wisconsin's north woods.

My thanks

To my lovely and loving, patient, brilliant partner in life, Pamela. To great Dads and buddies – in chronological order -- my sons Tony, Joe and Jake, my godsons Tony, Oscar and Louis and their 14 kids. What good fathers you are. To my beautiful, extraordinary daughter, Lauren.

To my Mom and Dad and my siblings, Tony, Steve, Mark, and Lynn, and many cousins, especially Annie, who helped with the memories and facts about our Grandfather Stanley. And to my extraordinary Grandparents.

Your warmth, humor and love make life worth everything.

Special thanks to the priests, nuns (all teachers), professors, and writers who encouraged, praised, copy-edited, confused, confounded, inspired, and berated me for the right reasons.

Writing is a team sport.

Introduction

On again, off again. Intermittent. Interminable. Life intervenes in strange and unpredictable ways – generally for the good, in my experience.

This book began more than 40 years ago with the earliest collection published as my Master's Thesis at Syracuse University. Some of those early works are included here, with my (hopefully, readers will agree) more mature work.

I paused my poetry when my plans for an academic career morphed into a career in public relations – an emerging profession that valued writing a bit more than most poetry publishers in 1975. (This, an early lesson in financial communications.) Pursuing my writing in the corporate world engaged all of my creative and analytic skills, often depleting all of my energy and zeal for my first love – poetry and fiction.

My personal writing also took a back seat to parenting, first as a single parent, then, a father of three and now four, with nine grandchildren. But, conscious choice or not, there were no trade-offs. Being a Dad is perhaps the most rewarding aspect of living, and at times, one of the most frustrating. Fatherhood is the inspiration for much of this book.

Thanks again to all those who have continued to encourage my writing – this is the first of many collections that I hope will inspire you as you have inspired me.

I. Beyond reach

sitting here
late when the quiet is deadly
I can hear leaves fall
against the chimney flue
each time a separate sound
easily heard
among the indiscriminant sounds
of the world

I know it is autumn
not by the coolness
in the house at night
but by the individual
sounds of leaves
dried and crackling
imitating the sounds
of split trees
which will soon burn
in that place

is it because I feel
old today
old, my mouth full of leaves
each of those fading colors
I'd wish to kiss
or is it weariness
hearing the seasons pass

perhaps my distance
in the midst of change
makes me stop and listen
to one leaf
by chance, entering
that black mouth

Poem for my grandfather

His clock sounds
every hour from nine to twelve
the other hours are seven minutes late
only one chime pealing.
The clock, veneer
curving over hardwood frame,
gears sluggish with dust
stands above his chair.
The chair, bent hickory and American pine
without give in the seat or back.

My grandfather, once mayor of
Pulaski, fought in the Argonne,
he says, showing old
wounds like photographs.
These moments he
lives for, the retelling.

Since nineteen fifty
the clock strikes late.
His children watch
an object falling
beyond reach.
His wound-out time
chimes so familiar,
and the man, alone it seems,
keeps his uncomfortable chair,
and cherishes a green cigar.

Craft

-- for Robert Duncan

The walls of my house
are made of glass or wind.
I view the airborne dust,
shifting debris, slowly etching
the glistening surface. Within
particles seem woven by perception,
natural, commonplace.

The loom treadles, affecting this space
like time; preconceptions
shuttle; metaphors escape
in the beauty of things.

The walls like glass cannot
like walls enclose me;
affected by winds, the
burgeoning load is buffeted,
is thought.

Within the trembling mind,
does the thought revolve around a
spindle, do I weave what I view
do I see the dust?

The walls of my house are
made of glass, or wind
the house contains the loom
I weave the cloth.

Saint Augustine Street in the summer

Sitting on your porch
you say your leg hurts when you walk,
so you don't walk much anymore.

The maples were replaced by a sidewalk and curb,
the porch grape arbor cut away,
where robins nested every summer
and we would count the blue eggs,
watch the young grow and fly.

We never found out what color eagle's eggs are,
you wouldn't let climb the tree near your cabin,
you said the nest was built of branches
the size of your arm.

You used to fly open-cockpit planes,
but gave me your leather helmet
ten years ago,
and last year you parted
too easily with your red hunting coat.
It was too heavy, you said.

I remember walking with you in the North Woods.
I complained about being tired,
you said you could walk with a bum leg
and you were 70 then.

We started going to bars when I was 14,
you told Grandma we were going for cigars and the mail.
At first you told your friends I was from the city,
now you say, "This is my grandson, who teaches
at the university." They were always impressed,
you always bought the beer.

I want to be with you,
shake energy into your tired limbs,

listen to your stories
and let you show me off at the Blue Moon Hotel and Bar.

See you rocking on the porch,
where we spent all too many summers
drinking mulberry juice in the shade,
watching blue shells crack
and wobbly young emerge.

Your bones

    -- for Georgia O'Keefe

After a thorough gnawing
cast-off bones are weathered dead dull,

pelvis with a view:
hip-socket, eyehole
of the bones of women
above a child's nesting
a buzzard circles
just out of view.

The sky passes through the pelvis
few can see the procession of
midwives and bearers, ashen-faced
wearing milky shifts.

Those who refused to submit
struggle with unclean
ingredients: bone, eye
of newt, bat's tongue,
a writing toad
to quench their fever.

Achy bones, the light they
absorb in their deadness
is abstracted,
stripped of meat
clutched in scrub-gnarled, arthritic hands,
softened by constant handling,
yet dignified in their new postures.

Croix de Guerre (green and red)

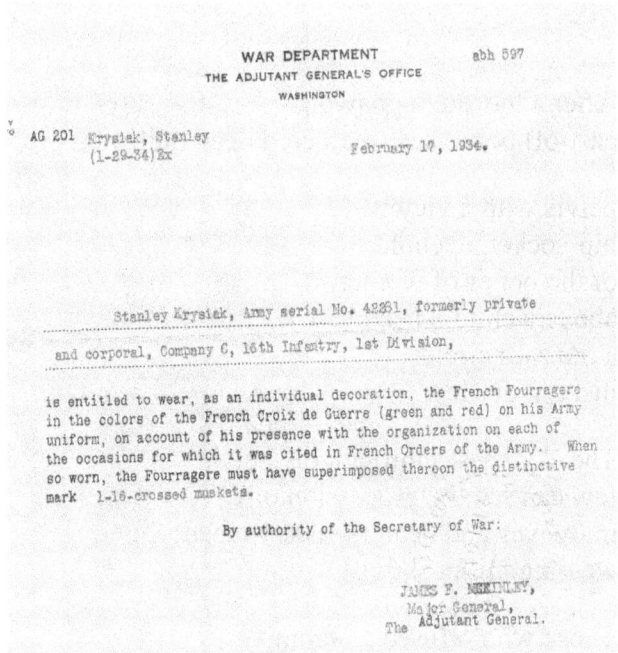

```
                          WAR DEPARTMENT            abh 597
                  THE ADJUTANT GENERAL'S OFFICE
                          WASHINGTON

  AG 201  Krysiak, Stanley
          (1-29-34)2x              February 17, 1934.


          Stanley Krysiak, Army serial No. 42261, formerly private

     and corporal, Company C, 16th Infantry, 1st Division,

  is entitled to wear, as an individual decoration, the French Fourragere
  in the colors of the French Croix de Guerre (green and red) on his Army
  uniform, on account of his presence with the organization on each of
  the occasions for which it was cited in French Orders of the Army.  When
  so worn, the Fourragere must have superimposed thereon the distinctive
  mark  1-16-crossed muskets.

                      By authority of the Secretary of War:


                              JAMES F. MCKINLEY,
                                 Major General,
                          The  Adjutant General.
```

Did you know
lying there
in a mud-filled trench
lifeless bodies splayed around you
passing from searing
pain to
unconsciousness
throbbing waking you again
and again
as your leg, arm and belly bled
mixing red with the muddy green grass and rain water
mustard gas wafting
fearful awake listening
for

German infantrymen casually

shooting heads
and hearts
the wounded
you, Army serial No. 42281,
the only survivor
corporal, Company C, 16th Infantry, 1st Division

Did you hear us calling over the decades

Did you dream of what could be

"Stanley...."

can you hear me

                    "I will
                    love
                    you forever"

                        "Damn stupid running
                        away to get shot"

Did you think you'd have two sons
a daughter

they   13 children
grandchildren   and   they
dozens more   great-grandchildren

only

if

you

live.

But how?

low moans   rifle shots   German voices

must muffle the pain

can't call out

"Stan -- ley"   "Don't you *dare* take that boy to any
bars
when you get the mail"

"Hey, Colonel Chicky. Who's the youngster?"

            "Chicago boy, my oldest grandson. We'll have
two nickel beers, Felix."

"Stan – ley!"

        "Pop"   "How about advancing your son a few
bucks on a Friday night?"

"Stanley"   "Let's honeymoon in Port Washington"

        "You're going to get caught making beer under the
chicken coop"

"It's a boy, Stanley"

"90 days in jail for making beer"

        "You've been elected Village President"

       "Let's name her Lorraine"

"Stanley, Junior"

        "Grandpa, can I sit on your lap?"

"Why are Robin's eggs blue?"

"What happened to your leg?"

"Why did you have to fight in a war?

"Will I have to go?"

New voices   not English

not

German   familiar
        Polish.

You whispered at first,
then cried out.

The two -- Polish Red Cross

Weeks in the hospital near Argonne
six months in Paris

       then home
shattered bone

    left leg four inches shorter
       elbow fused
little finger perpetually curled
    one kidney   "One's enough."

Did you know

the voices

    oddly remembered

13

as if in a dream

    calling you

        each of us

      never to exist

without you

       do.

      French Fourragere (green and red)

II. House of death

War dead

Your friends gambled for your new
sou'wester,
"There's no sense ruining it."
You complained that your footlocker
had been rifled, sextant removed.

Death was head-on,
the lead boat drawing fire.
No one could survive that mission,
in that blinding tropic sun.

You kept the sou'wester, and brought
the ship back.
You called your crew,
"The Unsung Heroes of the Pacific Theater."

The Army surgeon, occupied with wounds,
glanced over your charred face
diagnosing sun poisoning. You received
a Purple Heart.

He could not imagine unnatural growth,
the roving tumors leading to death,
twenty years after that last mission.

Finally, the blackness spread inside:
one lung, sounds on the left side,
croaking yes or no,
your wishes were recorded, not to donate
eyes now that one was blind,
no veteran's ceremonies so long after the war,
no open-casket horrors for the living.

You said, "It wasn't the Army surgeon's fault. It was the sun."

Twenty years dissolved
to death, delayed reaction,
your white eye like
blank sunlight on New Guinea waters
fusing war into skin.

Old wood, those memories

I know the wood you taught me to shape:
old cherry, maple and pine; carefully
sorted and stacked, hoarded for future use.

And delicately curved and joined chairs
arched, dovetailed cabinets and bureaus
you rebuilt, finished, arranged
around the walls of your house.

And the pleasure you took, and I found
in those pieces, old wood, plain designs
work done generations in the past.

I knew you were an artist; sketches, paintings
cartoons and ads framed scrapbook leaves
in your studio, your house.

I knew the conversations with your friends
musing over the past, retelling it for me,
I wanted to know who you were, father-in-law.

I learned your stories, jobs and places.
I mention them, as if they had become
my own experiences, ideas.

I cannot forget another man, when I was a child,
who brought black bread, candy and beer
to share with us, his family, laughing and
talking into the night.

That lonely man died when I was five, these few
things I remember: black bread still warm, candy, beer
and their absence, gone with the cancer that took him away.

I cannot forget the smell of decaying flesh that

you lived with for months, and your pain,
I could not imagine that pain.

I cannot forget the hand-worked wood and your stories,
your black bread, candy and beer,
I knew you briefly, not long enough.

no gentle rain falls
it rips a cataract
sending leaves and branches
into a heap of brown
twisted and glistening.

beneath, the hole
with ashes, square
of sod, green lost to
brown, the tiny grave.

strange, they had to
disturb the grass
work among the quiet worms
and pale grubs
to deposit dust.

kicking away the leaves
recalling raking the lawn
that he was no longer able
to rake, how he resisted
the slow passing.

gathering branches,
piling them on another
grave, carefully replacing
the yellow chrysanthemums
that had blown aside.

at Christmas, flowers gone,
an evergreen spray, called
a blanket,
covered that place.

the grass still
showed the cut plainly.
hoarfrost lipped

the edges, trapped
a single leaf.

perhaps they will plant
a blue spruce.
one clear flame beyond
the chiseled granite.

soon, spring will mend
the scar, the grass no
greener for hidden decay. He
will be lost from memory.

no gentle rain falls.

Elegy for Buck: Six-pointer

Driving from the valley to the city
I passed you, tied fender to fender
1960 Ford with rust holes under your head
red tag fluttering from your ear
past New York State Deer Check Station on Highway 20

Did they check your papers
can you enter the city
hang until your blood covers the ground
Did they notice heartbeat, respiration ended
or see two bullet holes
between your shoulder and neck
Did they ask your crime

Is this the proper way to celebrate
your death
Old Ford bearing you
penniless eyes in my read-view mirror
tail trickling red
on the hood,
smoking entrails
in some farmer's back yard

It was an overcast day
too cold to be riding outside
or walking, one slug knocked you down
getting up to fall once more
from Winchester's "30-odd-six"
dragged through wet leaves and snow
behind a grunting, sweating man
happy to fill his meat locker again

Visits to the house of death

-- Dedicated to the gracious old timers at St. Andrew's Home

The house was spotless, the marble floor
waxed so many times, chrome railings
polished step-by-step in the stairways.
Slowly, the chrome wearing to brass in places,
the gripping hands with brown spotted skin
barely concealing deep-blue veins,
the whiteness of tendon and bone.

Old clothes, repaired many times, pressed
and yet wrinkled; gabardine turned to sharkskin
over bodies bent and unable to fill it.
Nodding, shrunken heads with wisps of grey,
white hair; ever-present blue, dark veins
near the surface of skin.

Young, I walked quickly, not using elevators designed
to move slowly for hearts unable to resist
increased gravity, often passing someone
moving slowly up stairs. Later I would pass the
same person, a few steps farther, on
my way down.

Death is slow in those halls; they watch its
movements in mirrors. They hear it,
the low moans, the odor of old flesh, incontinence and stale clothes.
The house is full of that scent; overpowering as
I reach the infirmary.

I linger to read the bulletin board, messages: "thanks
for your prayers." Who will we pray for next?
Who will be carted to the ambulance, giving notice
belongings into the hall, obstacles
to remind the others, soon their things will
take their place.

Sepsis

The late caller
my sister.
"Dad's in the hospital. He went into shock, stopped breathing …
not doing well. I can't deal with these doctors and
nurses –
when can you get here?"

"On my way."

Book ticket. Drive to LGA before dawn. Park. Fly to Chicago,
connect to Greenbay. Rent car. Get lost on drive to hospital.
Park.

Meet sister in the ICU. "How is he?"
"How are you?"
"How's Mom?"
"What happened?"

"Oh, God. This is awful. He's dying."

The nurses' medical talk: "Septic shock. Vitals up and down.
Administering
massive doses of antibiotics. Not responding."

Then we learned about the "clinical trial" -- experimental chemo
"compromised resistance."

In his room I'm wearing a white shirt under a black sweater.
He's wired to translucent bags, ticking, flashing and chirping
behind him.
BP 180 over 110, pulse 109.

"Hi, Dad."

"Thanks for coming, Father. Ive been hoping you'd come -- think it's
time for the last rites."

"No, Dad, it's me. Your son."

Back into unconsciousness.

The gaggle of tubes,
sensors,
monitors bleeping, screaming.

Beep, scream, repeat. Again.
Blood oxygen 80.
Pulse 164, heart a frightened bird
defibrillating.

Nurses swoop in.
Injections.
Wait.
Watch.
Rest.

Repeat.

Finally, fitful
sleep.

The morning. The questions,
family
doctors.

Infection "arrested."
From near death, to
"home tomorrow."

Never the same. Trading dignity
for catheters, leg wraps,
infections, diapers, and

walkers.

Cancer returns. More infections.
Slowly shrinking from
sight.

A new life of dying begins.

Gauntlet

We entered the area
explorers walking trails
canoes stranded on rocky soil
sunlight blasting us
tumbling over portages
years of floral abuse
pine needles crumbling into humus
driftwood shattered on jagged granite
branches whip our faces
thorns pierce to bone
leaving the traces,
a natural design,
the withered limbs of trees.

We crossed against the wind
pitching tents on the lee side
sheltered by spruces warped by the bitter wind
cling to outcrops –
that glacial island.

We tried to avoid the larger animals
there is little food to support them here
we feared they would come against the waves
never having seen creatures like us before.

Once we heard a lark
but must have been mistaken
deaf from the wind
and the cries of loons.

Night fires out
eyes appeared
carnivores,
snorting in the dust and our scent,

moon never appearing
stars lost among the clouds.

Dreams of maggots under the hide
of a poached doe,
its woman's eyes, accusing,
stigmas in the frigid sky.

The morning was new air against my check
canvas slapped me awake
clouds of gnats already about my eyes
inhaled with every breath
my skin turning to leather
that cold morning, that first day.

Quetico Park

Water is crystal in
granite faceted by long
since melted glaciers. Sparse,
twisted scrub pine cling
to the topsoil of their
acid creation.

Animals gnaw the back,
hoard the seeds; seeds left
in pine-needle burrows
begin anew the twist,
cling, spin, hold,
of scrub pine. Nestling ducks,
loons, sheltered by submerged roots,
repay refuge with calls.

A three-month-thaw waterfall
feeds a finger lake;
the distant summer sun
heats the shimmering water
a few degrees warmer than air.

All stops; in the silence
laughter prevails.
Men in wool plaid
motor to the foot of
the waterfall, splash in the shallows,
haul canoes to the portage.
They linger to cast lures
into the bubbling pool.

They pack up, struggle through
pine, slipping on jagged rocks

they work their way to the
neighboring lake. A loon bobs
up from hiding, its strange
music begins.

Southold town dump

In the photograph
          camellias
  and dahlias
smell blue
     look
       black
and   not   black.

In the photograph
        or perhaps
   an abandoned shadowbox
  the gulls
      and terns walking
among
   discarded flowers
squawk
   and spit back.

They are fooled
      by the wooden
   seagull
      mounted on driftwood
   lying against
       the stained
and shattered
     porcelain tank.

They are attracted
       by
   one of their kind
and the
   flowers smell
grey
   and   black.

III. Is it love

Spirit in the dark

> "A spirit in the dark
> Moving, moving
> Higher, higher…"
>   -- Aretha Franklin

Light filtered by moon-tide
as calculated
as the uppermost rhythms of the sea.

Something alive
floating, slowly undulating
each stroke silent.

Thick water
enclosing blue flesh
eyes ears lungs throat;
a miniature water buffalo,
a dark footing.

I listen to soft heartbeats
quicker than ours;
I feel the somersaults
beneath your mother's
hard belly.

You must dream fantastic motions
between great rolling calms,
a twisted umbilical,
or flying in a warm typhoon.

What trauma
to dream our dreams,
cold air and jutting edges, screams
like machines driven through sunlight,
taped voices and televised faces,
the fear of moving in the dark.

Dream of gestation

-- for Susan

I wake and reach for my armpit,
searching for bats implanted there.
In my dream I had consented --
someone had to raise them –
and I was told
by a kindly old man
they would be soft and cuddly
nestled there, in soft flesh
beneath unsuspecting hair.

It was almost a loving task,
although I quickly became ambivalent –
who wouldn't –
with tiny bloodsuckers
drawing from that hot,
pulsing artery
so close to the heart.

They must be preserved
for the continuation
of a race.
There would be others like me,
waiting,
with strange flapping growths
beneath an arm.

Awake, I wanted them gone.
Reaching under my arm, foolishly,
like that scientist in the movie,
THE THING,
saying to the monster man-eating plant
(who hung men up like pork

and fed the tiny seed pods
from its hands their fresh blood),
"I understand you, and
welcome you to earth…."

Embarrassed, hand within armpit,
in the dark I looked to you
now six months pregnant,
still not knowing
how unsure one could feel
about something growing inside
that wasn't gone
when waking from a dream.

The roses, our love

-- For my love on your birthday

The forbidden flower is most beautiful
The common most sweet

Roses,
petals wildly opened by time's breezes,
witness: a simple task, bearing
you through the arched hallway, we
spill onto your sinuous brass and iron bed.
so it was, long ago.

Your question while we danced,
we moved to our new rhythm:
"What would you like now?"
Eyes met, bodies close, our love
sheet lightening before a Midwestern
summer storm. Our spring warmed
the bitter winter night.

My hand opened for yours, caressed your
proud cheek, quicksilver passion moved us.
Your soft fingertips glided, as mine
discovered the satin above your breasts,
slid to the waist of your antique robe.
Only the roses, the roses.

Tremors from the epicenter, concentric rings
melt our conversation, now a dialogue of curves.
Lips upon lips. My tongue a midmorning breeze

upon the dewy petals of your skin. The
landscape began to dance.

Memories intrude as wind suddenly shakes
glass panes. Our commingling
brought a downpour. Your tears a confession,
words unspoken, not our love but
memories that hurt.

Our beginning, the roses witness.
The answer to your question, a question.
Our love, our laughter, daisies in a bed
of roses, love, and the past between us.

We hunger, fear the first taste, then fear
hunger. A tango, a waltz, when does
the dancer become the dance, when dance, the
dancer? What beauty brings tears to the touch,
what touch compels fears to vanish?

Oh Love, our love, yes, love.

Is he gone?

-- For my brother Steve

It must be 15 years or more.
All that remain are
fragments of light.
He's not here, not anywhere,
only a ghost in my head,
bits of memories in a binder,
housing yellowing page protectors.

Where is he?
Why did he go?
Where are his ashes?

On NPR we hear
there are three stages of death --
gone, memories, and the death
of the last memory.

So my brother remains…
tiny little fragments of light,
electrons, positive and negative, flashing
synapses to neurons hidden under the bone.

Life only postpones the inevitable.
He's gone, but didn't die in a war.
They called it off as his draft group was about to board the train. No,
he died at the kitchen table feeding his son,
safe in a highchair.

His diaphragm,
then heart stopping,
no one to revive him, while
his wife took their daughters to school, returning
to a terrified baby son, and a husband
breathless.

What did she tell the children?

The house was sold, along with
his ice blue metal flake Corvette Stingray convertible.
The survivors moved on.
What's left is in my office,
old photos, a birth certificate, a diploma
should his daughter take it?

Or, will it only stir up old memories,
Tiny fragments of light
Neurons and electrons spinning as we try to sleep.

When Worlds Collide

-- For Jake, age three

It happens when the spider plant
makes shadows before your sleepy eyes.
"Spiders! Daddy. I dream spiders!"
("We all dream spiders.")

Sudden light makes our eyes blink
as we crawl on hands and knees, searching.
"No spiders here. None behind the bureau.
None under the radiator. None in the closet.
None under the bed."

Giggles.
"I dream spiders, Daddy!"

I dream spiders, too.
We all dream spiders. And watch the whirlpool
as water runs down the drain. We dream and
generation after generation, images overlap.
All fathers crawl.

Walking in the park next morning, you announce me
to everyone we meet. "That's my Daddy."
It reawakens my own childish proclaiming. The fear
and trembling at night. The deep-voiced reassurances.

Our worlds collide. I miss my father's few hugs.
I still dream spiders.

"Don't dream spiders. Dream hugs."

IV. Beginning

Fathers

> "In a new exposition of the Virgin's role, the Pope said:
> 'The modern woman will note with pleasant surprise that
> Mary of Nazareth, while completely devoted to the will of
> God, was far from being a timidly submissive woman or one
> whose piety was repellant to others.'" (*NY Times*, 3.22.74)

In her alcove, the Virgin glances,
eyes almost moist. The priest,
sweat glistening above his thin
slightly parted lips, grey thumbs
poised, anticipates: "My body, my blood."

"Any woman entering this place is asking
for it. Short skirts an open invitation.
Threatened by an open window or bed
They always comply. We take turns. At first
They fight, after the second time we insist
They enjoy it, and the tenth slides easily.
Afterwards, we offer them money."
         -- Frat house gang rapist, 1973

Her body, mysterious blue folds
willingly entered, immaculate mother.
That airy instant causing the weight of
gestation, her blood bursting with life.
Her husband loved her, but he didn't
believe, until an angel told him.

In the parking lot, breasts taunting,
legs lascivious within nylon, secret
mouth whispering, forcing lust and
suddenly beneath, spread-eagled, pummeled,
cries sound like, "More, more."

My father read me the facts of life from

a book called *Listen, Son.* "Women should be
placed on a pedestal, their needs provided for."
My mother, kneeling, scrubs white linoleum.
She doesn't want a career, she enjoys being
"treated like a lady."

We void ourselves, quick shudder in the groin,
Fitful emotions. We send our love shrieking,
Expanding our emptiness, we fill their spaces
with our seed, provide for their needs.

We are men.

Parochial

> Father and mother sit in state in the sitting-
> room perusing such papers only, as they are well
> assured have nothing carnal in them.
> -- Emily Dickenson, November 16, 1851

I threw you against the dining room wall
when I was 18. I have forgotten
the arguments in terms of insurance,
the anger over money. Your letters still
begin with questions of finance,
I still answer them.

Even after twelve years of parochial school,
I would find you looking through my books,
hiding those you thought were smutty.
Ulysses and *The Grapes of Wrath*.

You ask me why I couldn't write about less
serious things than sex and death. You still ask
if I go to mass. You know I never do.

My education was wasted, since I
lost my soul. You sold apples during the depression.
Apples were good for the soul. Everyone must have
life insurance, a solid investment, like
confession, mass and communion.

Ad Altare Dei

> "If you are late for mass three times in a row,
> you will be taken off patrol duty."
> -- Sister Mary Evangelista

I. The Mystery

We were all in the service of Christ
except for the girls, who were downstairs.
So we memorized the Latin service,
practiced the movements of the mass.

Intimidated by the scowling, red-faced pastor
who was soon to retire, there was something
wrong with his voice, I could hardly hear
his hoarse words.
I hoped the other kid would remember the lines.

The same old man and two women,
knelt in the front pews, waiting
for my mistakes at 6:30 a.m. mass.

The pastor already was angry, I had
spilled wine filling the cruets, dropped
my surplice in the hall (the sisters have
to wash them, son), and my shoes weren't polished.

I worried throughout the mass, would the
priest be angry since I already had breakfast
and couldn't take communion?

Finally, there was THE MYSTERY OF THE EUCHARIST:
One day the priest would drop a wafer,
and I would have to catch it, in the air.

II. Near Martyrdom

The sisters told us that Father K.,
who couldn't speak English well, had recently
escaped from Lithuania because the communists
were killing priests.

He made us dress him for mass,
reminding us that he was Christ's emissary
and in Lithuania the people knew how important
the priest was. He kissed each garment,
before putting it on.
We never wanted his blessing, because
he made us kneel as he disrobed.

We thought he curled his hair at night,
in those little rubber spools that women
used to make "spit-curls."
He was almost bald, and combed the curly fringe
towards his forehead.

We called him Father Spoolie.

He drank the most wine during mass.

III. Promotions

The sisters held lotteries to select servers
for funerals and weddings.
The older boys always won.

They would tell us how much money they got.

Weddings had more Latin, we worked hard for the money.
Funerals were like adoration,
without the monstrance, and less kneeling.
There was lots of incense, and when the censer
went out, we would return to the sacristy
to try to light some more.

At my first funeral, the sister changed her mind
and made me a pall-bearer, because it was a girl
from our grade that died and I was tall
for my age.
I didn't know her,
but we got to ride in a Cadillac and eat lunch in a restaurant.

We always had nightmares after funerals,
cold hands touching in the dark.

IV. Stick Matches

The sign of a good altar boy was how serious
he kept his face when lighting the candles
and during mass. We all carried stick matches
to light the candle-lighters in the sacristy.

When the wands went out at the altar we would have
to go back and re-light them, or let the other kid
finish both sides.

We had contests to see who could light the most candles
without his wand going out. Christmas and
Easter were the best because
there were twenty-four candles.

When the candles were lit, we began mass.
Between Latin we whispered jokes, trying to make
each other laugh out loud.

One time the pastor caught me.
He stopped the mass, said it was a sin to laugh
in church, and sent me home
without finishing.

Afterwards, I trembled
lighting candles, never smiling
in church.

I had "renounced
the glamour
of evil."

V. Body and Blood

Priests keep their own chalices
and the altar wine locked up
in a safe.
We would come early to try the combination before
the priest showed up.

The wine was made by brothers in California,
but it was yellow. We thought it changed to red
during communion. We never found out, because
the priests drank it all.

Once the pastor sent us with a note
for three bottles. We changed the number to four
on the way to the rectory.

We hid the fourth bottle in the furnace room
that connected the school and the church by
a tunnel. We would sneak between classes
and eat wafers and drink wine.

We never got caught, but one kid threw up
in Geography.

VI. More Mysteries

During communion, the priest
put the wafer in a lady's mouth,
but she didn't stick her tongue out far enough,
or it wasn't wet, so
the wafer fell.

I had the palate under her chin,
but when I moved to catch the wafer,
the palate slanted and the wafer fell to the floor.

The priest pushed me aside, picked it up
with his two blessed fingers, and ate it.
But there were tiny crumbs, so he took my palate
and place the crumbs and some dirt there.

He rushed into the sacristy, and I watched him
throw the crumbs down the sink.
He said the sink was blessed, and the water
didn't go to the sewer. It went to a tank
(which we figured had a gold lining, because
the Eucharist couldn't touch any other metal,
even silver) and was sent to the bishop's office
to be destroyed in
a special ceremony.

They thought of every detail.

VII. Regulations

In the sixth grade I had a fight
with another patrol boy while we were on duty.

He told Sister Evangelista I made his nose bleed
onto his new uniform shirt, and that I had strangled
him with his new tie.

She saw the dark red spots, and suspended me from patrol
for the rest of the term.

I quit serving.

IV. A taste of *Postcards to the Living*

weeping mulberry
leaves the shape
color
of Africa
none of us knew who planted it there, alongside
the red brick family house
nestled between maple and blue spruce

generations of us played within its ground-to-sky canopy
parting the leaves to hide and seek
within a bird's nest of interwoven branches

when the purple black berries were just about ripe,
Grandma woke us at sunrise
rubbing sleep from our eyes we plucked
the succulent midnight blue berries in a race
to best the swarming birds screeching at first light
angling for the fruit
Our reward
Grandma's homemade jam on whole wheat toast
cool sweet purple juice on a sweltering afternoon

decades of uncles, aunts, brothers and sisters, cousins slipped
through those sheltering branches a
movie set for
parents with cameras
black and white memories that
became color and then
deep green and shadows framing silent wondering
blue-eyed faces
above slight bodies clad in summer shirts and shorts

childhood past
we wept when
still healthy and bursting with fruit
it was cut down to expand
the old house

for what good reason?

all that was left
an armload of gnarled branches
we stripped away the bark
revealing bones tattooed with worm trails
perfect for our last Uncle to craft into lamps
posing in the corners of his living room

even at 90, he missed that mulberry
musing aloud
who cut it down

Not knowing it would be his last birthday we
planted a weeping mulberry sapling
climate-hardy for central Wisconsin
happy with a beloved companion
in his dying days
a reminder of so much more

our family tree

Postcards from Dean

How could you leave so abruptly
traveling with your daughter
end of semester present
clot stopping your heart in Prague
such an elegant city for dying

We were going to play golf
I didn't cancel the tee time
played with your memory

You still aimed left to correct
that slice
putts just missing the cup
scoring creatively.

So, is your new course nice
who walks with you when you walk
Mez, your Bichon Frise
happy to have you back
have you seen his pal
my late pup Valentino
on your strolls

You must have thought you were cured
of errant solids forming moving slowly thicker
up your leg
to your lungs, but
flying has risks
like
dying

I've been getting your postcards late at night
photos of undulating greens fairways
grinning Bichons
your latest money-making brainstorm

a wacky new driver guaranteed to hit straight (really, you
wrote)
in the background
a country estate
always out of focus
always with a pool
but not you

Keep the postcards coming
I'll keep reading them

good

for more than 20 years driving
south on Route 22
tiny yellow shed beckons
caught in the corner of my left eye
mysterious message in crude
chocolate block letters

    3G's
CoLLECTibLES

THiNK GooD
FEEL GooD
DO GooD

what could possibly be inside

and yet I'd never stopped
to explore
its mysterious treasures
instead intrigued
for miles
pondering
the meaning
the order of
commands
the mind that
painted them

About the Author

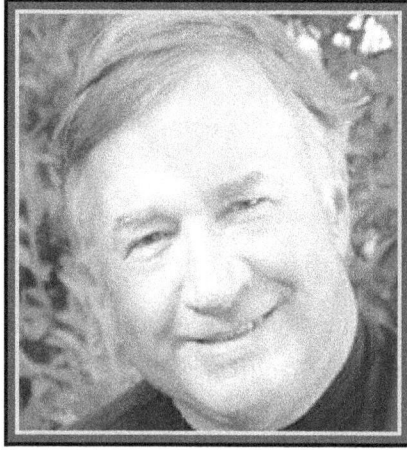

Ken Koprowski is a writer, communications consultant, and educator. His collection of poetry, *Fathers – Collected Poems 1973-2015,* was published by Ravenswood Publishing in the summer of 2016. In addition to being a prolific writer, he is an award-winning creative director and producer, and photographer. He earned his B.A. in English literature at the University of Illinois Chicago, as well as an M.A. in Creative Writing with a specialization in poetry, and completed his doctoral coursework at Syracuse University before pursuing a career in public relations. He is working on a second book of poetry, *Postcards to the Living,* a collection of short stories entitled *Draft Dodgers,* a play about his grandfather's experiences in WW I, and two non-fiction books.

He currently teaches writing and a range of public relations subjects in the communications Master's programs at New York University, Iona College and Manhattanville College. He teaches business communications courses he designed in the School of Business at UConn Stamford.

Ken has extensive advertising, marketing and communication management experience. He served as corporate spokesperson in diverse, complex and difficult situations. Ken has written speeches for many well-known corporate leaders, and drafted countless reports, Op-Eds, plans, ads, video and audio scripts, websites, blogs, and more. He recently edited, and wrote the introduction and chapter on using digital and social media for a popular crisis communications handbook.

Ken grew up in the Midwest – in Chicago and central and northern Wisconsin. For the past 40 years, he's lived and worked in New York, southwestern Connecticut and southern Vermont. He and his wife of 38 years raised three sons and a daughter, and they in turn have nine children, who keep them happy and very, very busy.

www.ingramcontent.com/pod-product-compliance
Lightning Source LLC
Chambersburg PA
CBHW071932020426
42331CB00010B/2828